Pastoral Letters

Pastoral Letters

by

Robert Murray McCheyne

A Collection of Ten Letters
Written in 1839

Shoals, Indiana

Pastoral Letters
PUBLISHED BY KINGSLEY PRESS
PO Box 973
Shoals, IN 47581
USA
Tel. (800) 971-7985
www.kingsleypress.com

ISBN: 978-0-9719983-1-5

Distributed in the UK by:
Harvey Christian Publishers UK
11 Chapel Lane
Kingsley Holt
Stoke-on-Trent, ST10 2BG
Tel. (01538) 756391
www.harveypublishers.co.uk
Email: sales@harveypublishers.co.uk

Credits:
Graphic design by Edward Cook

Printed in the United States of America

Contents

Foreword

To the best of my knowledge this little book is unique in at least two ways. First of all, this is the first time that Mr. McCheyne's Pastoral Letters have been printed separately from his other works. And secondly, this is the first time that the letters in their *original* form have been available to the public. The Pastoral Letters which have formed part of the *Memoir and Remains of Robert Murray McCheyne* since it was first published in 1844 were, according to its author, Andrew A. Bonar, somewhat revised by Mr. McCheyne for publication; whereas the letters in the present volume are reproduced as they were originally written by him and read by his congregation, to whom they were addressed.

I would like to take this opportunity of expressing my thanks to the Free Church of Scotland College, Edinburgh, for their kindness in providing me with typed copies of the original letters from their archives.

The letters as printed here are complete and unabridged. Some minor editing has, of necessity, taken place, but I stress that this has been minimal, and only with the view of bringing the text to be more in keeping with modern punctuation, spelling and usage. As this work is being published in the

United States of America, I have endeavored to follow American English spelling throughout, except when the author was either quoting from or paraphrasing the Scriptures—both of which he did frequently. All pronouns and other words obviously referring to Deity have been capitalized, including quotations from the Bible (which are are all from the King James Version).

It is greatly hoped that the publication of this small volume will bring these letters the attention they deserve from the Christian public, and that they will create a revived interest in the saintly McCheyne.

Edward Cook
Kingsley Press
February, 2003

Introduction

Robert Murray McCheyne was ill. For two years he had been the minister of St. Peter's Church in Dundee, Scotland. But a problem had developed with his heart, and his medical advisors recommended a period of complete rest in order to stop the condition spreading to his lungs. Accordingly he went to stay at the home of his parents in Edinburgh, thinking that he would be able to return to his beloved flock at St. Peter's within two weeks.

He was mistaken. His condition didn't improve, and he was obliged to remain in retirement for much longer than he had first anticipated. The twenty-five year old minister found it a great trial to be thus separated from his sphere of labor; for though he was so young, yet God's Spirit had wrought a deep work in his heart at conversion, and he was filled to an astonishing degree with the constraining love of Christ toward sinners. The fatherly love that he displayed toward his parishioners was also quite remarkable; and it was this concern for their welfare that led him, during this period of illness and attempted recuperation, to write the ten "pastoral letters" which make up this little book.

The letters thus written reveal a true pastor's heart. Though he could not be with his people in bodily presence, yet his heart yearned over them with a tender affection born of the love of God. His letters are full of exhortations to Christlikeness of spirit and holiness of heart and life. They reverberate with warnings to those still unconverted to flee to the Redeemer before it was too late. They were obviously written with the purpose of impressing upon the members of his congregation that although they were out of sight, they were still very much on his mind and in his heart. He didn't use the letters as an occasion to speak of himself, except to remind them that he was constantly praying for their spiritual welfare.

As the time of his illness lengthened out beyond his first expectations, the young minister began to see that God had specific reasons for withdrawing him from his congregation. In a letter dated January 18th, 1839, he expresses himself thus: "I sometimes think that a great blessing may come to my people in my absence. Often God does not bless us when we are in the midst of our labors, lest we shall say, 'My hand and my eloquence have done it.' He removes us into silence, and then pours 'down a blessing so that there is no room to receive it'; so that all that see it cry out, 'It is the Lord!'"

In this matter McCheyne proved to be right, for by the time he returned to take up his post later that year, God had wonderfully moved in revival blessing through the faithful ministry of another young minister by the name of William C. Burns. The godly McCheyne proved the genuineness of his love for souls and for the Kingdom of Christ by rejoicing in the blessings thus bestowed upon his congregation, even though it was through a channel other than himself. "I have no desire but the salvation of my people, by whatever instrument," was his comment.

Another reason he saw for God's temporarily removing him from his flock was so that his parishioners wouldn't make an idol out of him, and so that they would learn not to depend on him—their pastor—but on the Saviour Himself. Addressing this very issue, he wrote to one of his flock at Dundee: "A minister will make a poor saviour in the day of wrath. It is not knowing a minister, or loving one, or hearing one, or having a name to live, that will save. You need to have your hand on the head of the Lamb for yourselves (Lev. 1:4). You need to have your eye on the brazen serpent for yourselves (John 3:14-15). I fear I will need to be a swift witness against many of my people in the day of the Lord, that they looked to me, and not to Christ, when I preached to them."

In the providence of God, it was during this time of temporary retirement from his daily ministrations that the Church of Scotland decided upon a Mission of Inquiry into the state of the Jews. Four men were deputed to travel to the Holy Land and see what could be done in the interests of bringing the Gospel to the

Jews, and Mr. McCheyne was included in the number, as his medical advisors agreed that such a trip would in all likelihood be beneficial to his health. But even amidst the excitement, distractions and toil of foreign travel, his congregation at Dundee were not forgotten. And so it was that the last two pastoral letters which appear in the pages that follow were written while he was on this trip.

Robert Murray McCheyne died in his twenty-ninth year. His life was short, but its fragrance and influence lives on. "Live so as to be missed," was his advice to others, and in this he practised what he preached. Let his biographer and bosom friend, Andrew Bonar, tell us the secret of his spiritual success: "During the last years of his short life, [he] walked calmly in almost unbroken fellowship with the FATHER and the SON."

"He being dead yet speaketh."

[Those desiring to read the full biography of this unusual saint of God, as well as a collection of his letters, sermons and sacred songs, should obtain a copy of the *Memoir and Remains of Robert Murray McCheyne,* which is published by the Banner of Truth Trust.]

A calm hour with God is worth a whole lifetime with man.

LETTER ONE

To all of you, my dear friends, and people who are beloved of God and faithful in Christ Jesus, your pastor wishes grace and peace from God the Father, and Jesus Christ our Lord.

As several of you have expressed a desire to hear from me, and as He Who at the first sent me to you to bear witness of the Lord Jesus has for many weeks withdrawn me—and still lays His afflicting but gentle hand upon me—it has seemed good to me, not without prayer, to write to you from week to week a short word of exhortation. May the Holy Spirit guide the pen, that what is written may be blessed to your comfort and growth in grace.

"God is my record, how greatly I long after you all in the bowels of Jesus Christ"; and the walls of my chamber can bear witness how often the silent watches of the night have been filled up with entreaties to the Lord for you all. I can truly say with John that "I have no greater joy than to hear that my children walk in truth." And though many of you were in Christ before me, and were living branches of the True Vine long before I was sent in to the vineyard; yet believe me it is true of you also, I have no greater joy than to know that you are more and more filled with the Holy Ghost, and bear more and more fruit to the glory of God the Father. "Herein is My Father glorified, that ye bear much fruit."

You remember what Paul, when he was "a prisoner of the Lord," wrote to the Philippians: "I would ye should understand, brethren, that the things which happened unto me have fallen out rather unto the furtherance of the Gospel" (Phil. 1:12). I am very anxious that you and I should understand the very same in the things which have happened unto me, that we may vindicate God in all His dealings with us, and not despise the chastening of the Lord.

I know too well that there are many amongst you who would feel it no grievance if all the Lord's ministers were taken out of the way. Ah, how many are there who would rejoice if they were for ever left to sin unreproved, and to do what is right in their own eyes! Still I am quite sure that to you who have obtained like precious faith with us, to you who are the Lord's people, the present is a season of affliction, and you feel as Naomi felt—that "the hand of the Lord has gone out against us."

Still I would shortly persuade you that it is well—the Lord doeth all things well—and that it may be really for the furtherance of the Gospel amongst you. In many ways may this be the case.

1. With respect to myself. It does not become me here to show what benefit it may have on me. Suffice it to say that it has been a precious opportunity in which to reflect on the sins and imperfections of my ministry among you. A calm hour with God is worth a whole lifetime with man. Let it be your prayer that I may come out like gold, that the tin may be taken away, and that I may come back to you—if that be the will of God—a better man and a more devoted minister. I have much to learn, and these words of David have been often in my heart and on my lips: "I know, O LORD, that Thy judgments are right, and that Thou in faithfulness hast afflicted me" (Psa. 119:75). Ministers are God's tools for building up the Gospel temple. Now you know well that every wise workman takes his tools away from the work from time to time that they may be ground and sharpened. So does the Only Wise Jehovah take His ministers oftentimes away into darkness and loneliness and trouble, that He may sharpen and prepare them for harder work in His service. Pray that it may be so with your own pastor.

2. With regard to you, my dear brothers and sisters in the Lord, this time of trial is for your furtherance. Does not God teach you by means of it to look beyond man to the Saviour Who abideth ever? Is not God showing you that ministers are earthen vessels, easily broken, and fit only to be cast aside like a broken ves-

sel out of mind? Is He not bidding you look more to the treasure which was in them, and which flows in all its fullness from Christ? It is a sad error into which I see many Christians falling: that of leaning upon man—mistaking friendship toward a Minister for faith in the Son of God. Remember that before Moses was sent to deliver Israel, his hand was made leprous as white as snow, to teach them that it was not the might of that hand that could deliver Israel. It has been the fault of some of you to lean too much on man. Now God is teaching you that though the cistern may break, the fountain abides as open and full and free as ever; that it is not from sitting under any particular ministry that you are to get nourishment, but from being vitally united to Christ. Ministers are "not suffered to continue by reason of death. But this man [Christ], because He continueth ever, hath an unchangeable priesthood" (Heb. 7:23-24).

3. With regard to those among you who are almost but not altogether persuaded to be Christians, does not His Providence teach you to make sure of an interest in Christ without delay? You thought you would have the Saviour held up to you for an indefinite number of Sabbaths, little thinking that your Sabbaths and mine are all numbered. Many a time you have said to me in your heart, "Go thy way for this time; when I have a convenient season, I will call for thee." You did not think that a time might come when you may call

for your teachers and they be silent as the grave. I find many godly people here are expecting that a time will come when God's faithful witnesses shall be all put to silence, and anxious souls shall wander from sea to sea seeking the word of the Lord and shall not find it. Be entreated, oh wavering souls, to settle the question of your salvation now. Why halt ye between two opinions? It is most unreasonable to be undecided about the things of an endless eternity in such a world as this, with such frail bodies, with such a Saviour stretching out the hands, and such a Spirit of Love striving with you. Remember you are flesh. You will soon hear your last sermon. "I call heaven and earth to record this day against you, that I have set before you life and death, blessing and cursing: therefore choose life, that both thou and thy seed may live" (Deut 30:19).

4. There is another class, who are not of you, and are yet on every hand of you, "Of whom I have told you often, and now tell you even weeping, that they are the enemies of the cross of Christ: whose end is destruction, whose God is their belly, and whose glory is in their shame, who mind earthly things" (Phil. 3:18-19). Ah, you would not believe if I were to tell you the great heaviness and continual sorrow that I have in my heart for you. And yet I do hope that my absence may be blessed to you. Just think for a moment, if God were to remove your teachers one by

one; if He were to suffer the church of our Covenanted fathers to fall before the hands of her enemies; if He were to suffer Popery again to spread its dark and deadly shade over the land—where would you be? You that despise the Sabbath, that care little for the preached word; you that have no prayer in your families, and seldom in your closets; you that are lovers of pleasure; you that wallow in sin—you would have your wish then. You would have your silent Sabbaths indeed; no warning voice to cry after you; no praying people to pray for you; none to check you in your career of wickedness; none to beseech you not to perish. Learn, from so small a circumstance as the absence of your stated minister, what may be in store for you, and flee now from the wrath to come. It may be ye shall be hid in the day of the Lord's anger.

Finally, my dearly beloved and longed for, my joy and crown, abide all the more in Christ because of my absence. Maintain a closer walk with God, so that when I return—as God gives me now good hope of doing—I may rejoice to see what great things God has done for your souls. God feeds the wild flowers on the lonely mountainside without the help of man, and they are as fresh and lovely as those that are daily watched over in our gardens. So God can feed His own planted ones without the help of man, by the secretly falling dew of His Spirit. How I long to see you walking in holy communion with God in the world! I will never rest nor give God rest till He make you as a lamp that burneth, a city set upon a hill that cannot be hid.

Now strive together with me in your prayers to God for me, that I may come unto you with joy by the will of God. The grace of our Lord Jesus Christ be with you. My love be with you all in Christ Jesus. Amen.

Dated: *Edinburgh, 30 January, 1839*

Let every new sight of your wicked heart, let every new wave of trouble drive your soul to hide in Him, the Rock of your Salvation.

LETTER TWO

To all of you, my dear flock, who have chosen the good part which cannot be taken away, your pastor wishes grace, mercy and peace from God our Father, and the Lord Jesus Christ.

The sweet singer of Israel begins one of his Psalms with these remarkable words: "I will sing of mercy and judgment: unto Thee, O LORD, will I sing." This is the experience of all God's servants in time of trouble. Even in the wildest storms the sky is not all dark. And so in the darkest dealings of God with His children, there are always some bright tokens for good. His way with us of late has been "in the sea, and His path in the deep waters"; yet some of you may have felt that His own hand was "leading us like a flock."

One great token of His loving kindness has been the way in which He has supplied the absence of your stated minister. Ordained messengers, men of faith and prayer, have spoken to you from Sabbath to Sabbath in the name of the Lord. Awakening, inviting, comforting messages you have had. And even your meeting on Thursday evenings He has continued to you. The gates of the House of Prayer, like the gates of the City of Refuge, have been open to you, as ever inviting you to enter in and behold by faith what Jacob saw in Bethel—"the ladder set up on the earth, and the top of it reaching unto heaven"—inviting you to meet with Him with Whom Jacob wrestled till the breaking of the day. Think how often, in times of persecution, the Apostles were constrained to leave the seed they had sown, without leaving any one to water it but the Lord on Whom they believed. How often, in times of persecution in the Church of Scotland, our faithful pastors had to leave their few sheep in the wilderness, without any human shepherd to care for their souls, commending them to God and to the word of His grace. These times may come again. God may be preparing us for such fiery trials. But He hath not yet dealt so with us. He that tempers the wind to the shorn lamb, and Who "stayeth His rough wind in the day of His east wind," has mingled mercy with judgment; and even when He humbles us, gives us cause for praise. "Oh that men would praise the Lord for His goodness, and for His wonderful works to the children of men."

Another mark of His loving kindness to us is His suffering me to pray for you. You remember how the Apostles describe the work of the ministry: "We will give ourselves continually to prayer, and to the ministry of the word" (Acts 6:4). Now God is my record that this has been my heart's desire ever since my coming among you. I have always felt myself a debtor to you all, both to the wise and to the unwise; so as much as in me is, I have been ready to preach the Gospel unto you. But God has for a time withdrawn me from that part of the work amongst you. To me that grace is not now given—to preach among you the unsearchable riches of Christ. (Ah, how great a grace it is, how wonderful that it should ever have been given to me.) Still He allowed me to give myself unto prayer. Perhaps this may be the chief reason of my exile from you, to teach me what Zechariah was taught in the vision of the golden candlestick and the two olive trees (Zech. 4); that it is not by might, nor by power, but by His Spirit obtained in believing, wrestling prayer that the temple of God is to be built in our parishes.

I have hanged my harp upon the willows, and am no more allowed to "open to you dark sayings upon the harp," nor to "speak of the things which I have made touching the King," Who is "fairer than the children of men." Still my soul does not dwell in silence. I am permitted to go in secret unto God my exceeding joy. And while meditating His praise, I can make mention of you all in my prayers, and give thanks for the little flock who by patient continuance in well doing seek for glory and honour and immortality. "If I forget thee, O Jerusalem, let my right hand forget her cunning. If I do not remember thee, let my tongue cleave to the roof of my mouth; if I prefer not Jerusalem above my chief joy."

I feel that it is another gift of grace that I am suffered to write to you. You remember how often the Apostles cheered and strengthened the disciples, when absent from them, by writing to them. What a precious legacy to the Church in all ages have these Epistles been—every verse like the branches of the tree of life bearing all manner of fruit, and the leaves for the healing of the nations. You remember how the holy Samuel Rutherford, and many of our persecuted forefathers in the Church of Scotland, kept the flame of grace alive in their deserted parishes by sending them words of counsel, warning and encouragement—testifying, not face to face, but with ink and pen, the Gospel of the grace of God. I do feel it a great privilege that this door is opened to me; and that even when absent, I can oft speak to you of the things pertaining to the Kingdom. "This second epistle, beloved, I now write unto you; in both which I stir up your pure minds by way of remembrance." "Yea, I think it meet, as long as I am in this tabernacle, to stir you up by putting you in remembrance."

1. Abide in Him, little children, Whom I have always presented unto you, that when He shall appear, we may have confidence and not be ashamed before Him at His coming. Let every new sight of your wicked heart, let every new wave of trouble drive your

soul to hide in Him, the Rock of your Salvation. There is no true peace but in a present hold upon the Lord our righteousness.

2. Enjoy the forgiveness of sins. Keep yourselves in the love of God. If you abide in Christ you shall abide in His love. Your joy let no man take from you. These things write I unto you that your joy may be full.

3. Be ye clean that bear the vessels of the Lord. He that saith He abideth in Him ought himself so to walk even as He walked. Ah, how many falls will I have to mourn over among you when I return, if God send me back to you; how many unseemly quarrellings and miscarriages among you that are God's own; how many unlovely tempers amongst those who follow Him Who is altogether lovely. Oh take heed! Do not give the enemy cause to blaspheme. Naming the name of Christ, depart from all iniquity.

4. Continue in prayer. How many messages have been carried to you publicly and from house to house, and yet how little success. I bless God for all the tokens He has given us that the Spirit of God is not departed from the Church of Scotland, that the Glory is still in the midst. Still the Spirit has never yet been shed on us "abundantly." The many absentees in the forenoon of the Sabbaths, the thin meetings on Thursday evenings, the absence of men from all meetings for the worship of God, the few private prayer meetings, the little love and union among Christians—all show that

the plentiful rain has not yet fallen to refresh our corner of the heritage. Why is this? This is the day of Christ's power. Why are the people not made willing? Let James give the answer: "Ye have not because ye ask not." Hitherto have ye asked nothing in My name. Ask and ye shall receive, that your joy may be full.

Finally, dear brethren, farewell. Day and night I long to come to you, but still God hinders me. Do not omit to praise Him for all the great grace He has mingled in our cup of bitterness. Seven times a day do I praise Thee for Thy righteous judgment. When passing through the waters, He has been with us; and the rivers, they have not overflowed us; and therefore we may be sure that when we pass through the fires we shall not be burned, neither shall the flame kindle upon us.

Now may the God of peace Himself give you peace always by all means, and the grace of the Lord Jesus be with your spirits. Amen.

Dated: *Edinburgh, 6 February, 1839*

Affliction will certainly *purify a* believer.

LETTER THREE

*To all of you, my dear friends, and people who are and
shall ever be followers of the Lamb whithersoever He
goeth, your pastor again wishes grace and peace from
God our Father, and the Lord Jesus Christ.*

I long very much that this grace may again be given
unto me—to preach among you, face to face, "the
unsearchable riches of Christ." Oftentimes I purpose
to come unto you, but am let hitherto. Still I feel it a
great privilege that even in my retirement I can send
you a word to the end that you may be established. I
feel as if one door was left open to me by the Lord.
Believe me, it is the foremost desire of my heart that
Christ may be glorified in you, both now and at His
coming; that you may be a happy and a holy people,
blessed and made a blessing.

For the sake of variety, let me guide your thoughts
to a passage of God's own Word, and then I will speak
to you as if I were yet present with you, and half forget
that you are not before me.

In Job 23:8-10 you will find these solemn words:
"Behold, I go forward, but He is not there; and backward, but I cannot perceive Him. On the left hand,
where He doth work, but I cannot behold Him: He

hideth himself on the right hand, that I cannot see Him. But He knoweth the way that I take: when He hath tried me, I shall come forth as gold."

You all know the afflictions which came upon Job. He was a perfect and upright man, and the greatest of all the men of the East. Yet he lost his oxen and asses, his sheep and camels, and his ten children, in one day. Again the breath of disease came upon him, and he sat down among the ashes. In all this Job sinned not with his lips. He blessed the hand that smote him. "What? shall we receive good at the hand of God, and shall we not receive evil?" And yet when his troubles were *prolonged,* he knew not what to think. Learn how weak the strongest believer is; a bruised reed without Christ we are, and can do nothing. When Job's brethren dealt deceitfully with him as a crook; when he felt God hedging him in, and God's arrows drinking up his spirit; then clouds and darkness rested on his path. He could not unravel God's dealings with his soul. Then he cried, "Shew me wherefore thou contendest with me." He longed to get an explanation from God. "Oh that I knew where I might find Him! that I might come even to His seat!... Behold, I go forward, but He is not there; and backward, but I cannot perceive Him: on the left hand, where He doth work, but I cannot behold Him: He hideth Himself on the right hand, that I cannot see Him."

You have here then, in verses 8-9, a child of light walking in darkness—an afflicted soul seeking and seeking in vain to know why God is contending with him. Dear friends, this is not an uncommon case. Even to some of you, Job's providence often appears inexplicable. I hear that God has been at work among you, and "His way is in the sea." He has tried you in different ways: some of you by loss of your property as he tried Job; some of you by the loss of dear friends; some by loss of health, so that "wearisome nights are appointed you"; some by the loss of the esteem of friends—aye even of Christians—"your inward friends abhor you." Perhaps more than one trouble has come on you at a time, wave upon wave, thorn after thorn. Before one wound was healed, another came. Before the rain was well away, "the clouds returned." You cannot explain God's dealings with you. You cannot get God to explain them. You have drawn the Saviour's blood and righteousness over your soul, and you know that the Father Himself loves you. You would like to meet Him to ask, "wherefore contendest Thou with me?" "Oh that I knew where I might find Him."

My dear afflicted brethren, this is no strange thing that has happened unto you. Almost every believer is at one time or another brought to feel this difficulty. "God maketh my heart soft, and the Almighty troubleth me." Is it in anger, or is it in pure love that

He afflicts me? Am I fleeing from the presence of the Lord, as Jonah did? What change would He have wrought in me? If any of you are thinking thus in your heart, pray over this word in Job. Remember the word in Psalm 46, "Be still and know that I am God." God does many things to teach us that He is God and to make us wait upon Him.

And still further, see in verse 10 what light breaks in upon our darkness. But "He knoweth the way that I take: when He hath tried me, I shall come forth as gold."

1. Observe, "He knoweth the way that I take." What sweet comfort there is in these words! He that redeemed me, He that pities me as a Father, He who is the only wise God, He whose name is Love, *He* knoweth the way that I take.

The ungodly world do not know it. The world knoweth us not, even as it knew Him not. A stranger doth not intermeddle with the joys or with the sorrows of a child of God. When the world looks on your grief with unsympathizing eye, you feel very desolate; "your soul is exceedingly filled with the scorning of those that are at ease." But why should you? He that is greater than all the world is looking with intensest interest upon all your steps.

The most intimate friends do not know the way of an afflicted believer. Your spirit is lonely even among God's children; for your way is hid, and the Lord hath hedged you in. Still be of good cheer, the Father of all the best of friends knows well the way that you take.

You do not know your own way. God has called you to suffer, and you go like Abraham, not knowing whither you go. Like Israel going down into the Red Sea, every step is strange to you. Still be of good cheer, sufferer with Christ; God marks your every step. "The steps of a good man are ordered by the LORD: and He delighteth in his way." He that loves you with an infinite, unchanging love is leading you by His Spirit and Providence. He knows every stone, every thorn in your path. Jesus knows your way. Jesus is afflicted in all your affliction. "Fear not: for I have redeemed thee, I have called thee by thy name; thou art Mine. When thou passest through the waters, I will be with thee; and through the rivers, they shall not overflow thee: when thou walkest through the fire, thou shalt not be burned; neither shall the flame kindle upon thee" (Isa. 43:1-2).

2. "When He hath tried me, I shall come forth as gold." This also is precious comfort. There will be an end of your affliction. Christians must have "great tribulation," but they come out of it. We must carry the cross—but only for a moment—then comes the crown. I remember one child of God saying that if it were God's will that she should remain in trials a thousand years, she could not but delight in His will.

But this is not asked of us. We are only called *"to suffer a while."* There is a set time for putting into the furnace, and a set time for taking out of the furnace. There is a time for pruning the branches of the vine, and there is a time when the husbandman lays aside the pruning hook. Let us wait His time. He that believeth shall not make haste. God's time is the best time.

But shall we come out the same as we went in? Oh no! "We shall come out like gold." It is this that sweetens the bitterest cup. This brings a rainbow of promise over the darkest cloud. Affliction will *certainly* purify a believer. How boldly he says it, "I *shall* come out like gold." Ah, how much dross is there in every one of you dear believers, and in your pastor. "When I would do good, evil is present with me." Oh that all may be left behind in the furnace. What imperfection! What sin mingles with all we have ever done! But are we really fruit-bearing branches of the True Vine? Then it is certain that when we are pruned, we shall bring forth more fruit. We shall come out like gold. We shall shine more purely as "a diadem in the hand of our God." We shall become purer vessels to hold the sweet-smelling incense of praise and prayer. We shall become holy, golden vessels for the Master's use in time and in eternity.

To the many among you who have no part nor lot in Christ, I would say, see here the happiness of being a Christian in time of trouble. It is no small joy to be able to sing Psalm 46 in the dark and cloudy day. I have often told you, and now tell you when I am far from you: "We are journeying to the place of which the LORD said, I will give it you: come thou with us, and we will do thee good: for the LORD hath spoken good concerning Israel."

Finally, pray that your pastor may come out of his trials like gold. "All is not gold that glitters." Pray that everything that is but glittering dross may be taken away, and that if it be His will, I may come unto you like the fine gold of Ophir.

"Continue in prayer, and watch in the same with thanksgiving; withal praying also for us, that God would open unto us a door of utterance, to speak the mystery of Christ." My chief comfort concerning you is that "My God shall supply all your need according to His riches in glory by Christ Jesus." "Brethren, farewell. Be perfect, be of good comfort, be of one mind, live in peace; and the God of love and peace shall be with you."

The grace of the Lord Jesus Christ, and the love of God, and the communion of the Holy Ghost, be with you all. Amen.

Dated: *Edinburgh, 13 February, 1839*

Do not be discouraged, dearly beloved. . . because He does not seem to answer your prayers. . . . Perhaps your prayers will come back like the ships of the merchant—all the more heavily laden with blessings because of the delay.

LETTER FOUR

To all of you, my dear flock, who are chosen in Christ before the foundation of the world to be holy and without blame before Him in love, your pastor again wishes grace and peace from God the Father and our Lord Jesus Christ.

There are many sweet providences happening to us every day if we would but notice them. In the texts which ministers choose, what remarkable providences God often brings about. I have often felt this, and never more than now. Some of you may remember that the last chapter of the Bible which I read to you in the church was 1 Kings 19. There we are told of Elijah going away into the wilderness for 40 days and 40 nights to the mount of God, where he was taught that it is not by the wind or the earthquake or the fire that God corrects souls, but by the still small voice of the Gospel. May not this have been graciously intended to prepare us for what has happened?

Another providence some of you may have noticed: for several Thursday evenings before I left you, I was engaged in explaining and enforcing the sweet duty of believing prayer. "I was with you in weakness, and in fear, and in much trembling." Has not God since taught us the use of these things? "Trials make the promise sweet. Trials give new life to prayer." Perhaps some of us were only receiving the information into the head; is not God now driving us to practise the things which we learned?

I do not now remember all the points I was led to speak upon to you; but one, I think, was entirely omitted—I mean the subject of answers to prayer. God left it for us to meditate on now. Oh, there is nothing that I would love you to be more sure of than this: that God hears and answers prayer. There never was and never will be a believing prayer left unanswered.

Meditate on this, and you will cry, "I love the LORD, because He hath heard my voice and my supplications" (Psa. 116:1).

1. God often gives the very things His children ask, at the very time they ask it. You remember Hannah. She prayed in her heart for a man child, and the Lord remembered her and granted her petition that she had asked of Him; and she called his name Samuel—that is—"Asked of God." Oh that you could write the same name upon all *your* gifts. You would have far more joy in them, and far larger blessing along with them. You remember David in the 138th Psalm: "In the day when I cried Thou answeredst me, and strengthenedst me with strength in my soul."

You remember Elijah: "O Lord my God, I pray Thee, let this child's soul come into him again. And the Lord heard the voice of Elijah; and the soul of the child came into him again, and he revived" (1 Kings 17:21). You remember Daniel: "While I was speaking, and praying, and confessing my sin and the sin of my people Israel, and presenting my supplication before the Lord my God for the holy mountain of my God; *yea, while I was speaking in prayer,* even the man Gabriel, whom I had seen in the vision at the beginning, being caused to fly swiftly, touched me." Oh what encouragement is here for those among you who, like Daniel, are greatly beloved, to expect answers while you are speaking in prayer! Pray and look up.

You remember in Acts 12 the Church prayed without ceasing for Peter, who was cast into prison, and the answer surprised them at the door. Oh what surprises of goodness and grace God has in store for you and me if we only pray "without ceasing." If you will pray in union to Jesus—having childlike confidence toward God—having the Spirit of adoption crying Abba within you—seeking the glory of God more than all personal benefits, I believe that in all such cases you will get the very thing you ask at the very time you ask it. Before you call, God will hear; and while you are speaking, He will answer. Oh, if there were twenty among you who would pray thus, and persevere therein like wrestling Jacob, you would get whatsoever you ask. Yea, the case of Daniel shows that the prayer of one such believer among you will avail much. Delight thyself in the Lord, and He shall give thee the desires of thy heart.

2. God often delays the answer to prayer for wise reasons. The case of the Syrophenician woman will occur to you all. How anxiously she cried, "Have mercy on me, O Lord." But Jesus answered not a word. Again and again she prayed, and got no gracious answer. Her faith grew stronger by every refusal, till Jesus could refuse no longer, "O woman, great is thy faith; be it unto thee even as thou wilt." My dear praying people, "continue in prayer, and watch in the same with thanksgiving."

"The answer may be long delayed, but cannot come too late." You remember in the parable of the importunate widow—it is said that God *"bears* long with His own elect which cry day and night unto him." He hears all their prayers; He treasures them up from day to day, and soon the full answer will come down. The praying souls beneath the altar in Revelation 6:10 seem to show the same truth, that a believer's prayers may be answered even after he is dead. And again in that wonderful passage, Revelation 8:3, it is said that the Saviour, the great Intercessor with the Father, offers to God the incense of His merits "with the prayers of *all saints* upon the golden altar which is before the throne." Christ never loses one believing prayer. The prayers of every believer—from Abel to the present day—He heaps upon the altar from which they are continually ascending before His Father and our Father; and when the altar can hold no more, the full answer will come down. Do not be discouraged, dearly beloved, because God bears long with you— because He does not seem to answer your prayers. When the merchant sends his ships to distant shores, he does not expect them to come back richly laden in a single day. He has great patience. It is good that a man should both hope and quietly wait for the salvation of God. Perhaps your prayers will come back like the ships of the merchant—all the more heavily laden with blessings because of the delay.

3. God often answers your prayers by terrible things. So it says in the 65th Psalm: "By terrible things in righteousness wilt Thou answer us." And all of you who are God's children have found it true. Some of you have experienced what John Newton did when he wrote that beautiful hymn, "I asked the Lord that I might grow." Some of you, perhaps, have prayed, "Lord, increase my faith." In answer to this, God has shown you the misery of your connection with Adam. He has revealed the hell that is in your heart. You are amazed, confounded, abased. You cry, "Oh wretched man! Who shall deliver me?" You cleave to a Saviour God with a thousand times greater anxiety. Your prayer is answered. Your faith is increased.

Some of us prayed for a praying spirit. God has laid affliction upon us. Waves and billows go over us; we cry out of the depths. Being afflicted we pray—our prayer is answered "by *terrible things.*"

4. God often answers your prayers by giving something better than you ask. An affectionate father often does this. The child says, "Father, give me this fruit." "No my child," the father replies, "but here is bread, which is better for you." Paul felt a thorn in his flesh. With all his heart he cried, "Lord, let this depart from me." Three times he prayed, and what was the answer? Something better than he asked—it was sufficient grace. "My Grace is sufficient for thee." Dear praying believers, be of good cheer; God will either give what you ask, or something far better. Are you not quite willing that He should choose for you and me? You remember that even Jesus prayed, "Let this cup pass from Me." That desire was not answered, but "there appeared an angel from heaven, strengthening Him." He received what was far better—strength to drink the cup of vengeance.

Some of you, my dear believing flock, have been praying that if it be God's will I might be speedily restored to you, that God's name might be glorified. I have been praying the same. Do not be surprised if He should answer our prayers by giving us something above what we imagined. Perhaps He will glorify Himself by us in another way than we thought.

"Oh the depth of the riches both of the wisdom and knowledge of God." "Of Him, and through Him, and to Him, are all things."

These things I have written that you may have greater confidence in coming to the throne of grace. The Lord make you a praying people. Strive together in your prayers to God for me. I thank my God upon every remembrance of you, always in every prayer of mine for you all making request with joy. Now the God of patience and consolation grant you to be like-minded one toward another according to Christ Jesus. The God of hope fill you with all peace and joy in believing. And the God of peace be with you all. Amen.

Dated: *Edinburgh, 20 February, 1839*

Most of God's people are contented to be saved from the hell that is without; *they are not so anxious to be saved from the hell that is* within.

LETTER FIVE

*To all of you, my dear flock, who are washed and sanc-
tified and justified in the name of the Lord Jesus and
by the Spirit of our God, your pastor again wishes grace
and mercy and peace.*

This is now the fifth time I am permitted by God
to write to you. If you are not wearied, it is pleasant and refreshing to me. I wish to be like Epaphras,
"Always labouring fervently for you in prayers, that
ye may stand perfect and complete in all the will of
God" (Col. 4:12). When I am hindered by God from
laboring for you in any other way, it is my heart's joy to
labor for you thus. Dr. Scott of Greenock, a good and
holy minister, was laid aside by old age from preaching
for some years before his death. He used to say, "I can
do nothing for my people now but pray for them, and
sometimes I feel that I *can* do that." This is what I
also love to feel. Often I am like Emelia Geddie, who
lived in the time of the Covenanters, and of whom I
used to tell you: "The great part of my time is taken
up with bringing my heart to a tune for prayer." But
when the blessed Spirit does help my infirmities, it is
my greatest joy to lay myself and you my flock in His
hand, and to pray that God may yet make "the vine
to flourish and the pomegranate to bud."

If you turn to Isaiah 5:4 you will find these affecting words: "What could have been done more to my vineyard, that I have not done in it? Wherefore, when I looked that it should bring forth grapes, brought it forth wild grapes?"

Consider these words, my dear people, and may the Spirit breathe over them, that they may savingly impress your souls. These words are God's pathetic lamentation over His ancient people, when He thought of all that He had done for them, and of the sad return which they made to Him. We have come into the place of Israel. The branches of the olive tree have been broken off, and we have been grafted in. All the advantages God gave to Israel we now enjoy. And ah! has not God occasion to take up the same lamentation over us? I would wish each of you seriously to consider "what more God could have done to save your soul that He has not done." And oh, consider again whether you have borne grapes, or only wild grapes.

1. Consider what God has done to save your soul.

(i) He has provided a great Saviour and a great salvation. He did not give man or angel but the Creator of all to be the substitute of sinners. His blood is precious blood. His righteousness is the righteousness of God. And now, "To him that worketh not, but believeth on him that justifieth the ungodly, his faith is counted to him for righteousness" (Romans 4:5). Most precious word! Give up your toil, self-justifying soul. You go from mountain to hill seeking rest but finding none. Work not. What then? Believe the record that God hath given concerning His Son. A glorious, loving, all perfect, all divine Surety is laid down at your feet. He is within your reach. He is nigh thee. Take Him and live. Refuse Him and perish. "What could have been done more for my vineyard, that I have not done in it?"

(ii) Again, consider the ordinances God has given you. He has made you into a vineyard. Scotland is the likest of all lands to God's ancient Israel. How wonderfully has God planted and maintained godly ministers in it, from the time of Knox to the present day. He has divided the whole land into parishes. Even on the barren hills of our country, He has planted the choicest vine. Hundreds of godly laborers He has sent to gather but the stones of it. God has done this for you also. He has built a tower in the midst of you, and a winepress therein. He has sent me among you, who am less than the least of all the ministers of Christ, and yet "determined to know nothing among you, save Jesus Christ, and Him crucified." Has not the Spirit of God been sometimes present in our sanctuary? Have not some hearts been filled with gladness more than if corn and wine abounded? Have not some tasted "a love that is better than wine"? "What could have been done more for My vineyard that I have not done in it?"

2. Now let me ask, what fruit have we borne— grapes, or wild grapes? Ah, I fear the most can show

nothing but wild grapes. If God looks down upon us *as a parish,* ah! what does He see? Are there not still a thousand souls strangers to the House of God? How many does His holy eye now rest upon who are seldom in the House of Prayer—who neglect in the forenoon? How many who frequent the tavern on the Sabbath day? Ah, why do they bring forth wild grapes?

If God looks upon you *as families,* how many prayerless families does He see? How often have I listened, as I passed your windows, for the melody of Psalms—and listened all in vain! God also has listened, but still in vain. How many careless parents does His pure eye see among you who will one day, if you turn not, meet your neglected children in an eternal hell! How many undutiful children! How many unfaithful servants! Ah, why such a vineyard of wild grapes?

If God looks on you *as individual souls,* how many does He see that were never awakened for your soul? How many that never shed a tear for their perishing soul? How many that were never driven to pray? How many that know not what it is to bend the knee? How many that have no uptaking of Christ and are yet at ease? How many does God know among you that have never laid hold of the only sure covenant? How many have no "peace in believing," and yet cry "Peace, peace, when there is no peace"? How many does God see among you who have no change of heart, who are given up to the sins of the flesh and of the mind? Ah, why do you bring forth nothing but wild grapes—grapes of Sodom and clusters of Gomorrah?

Ah, remember you will blame yourself to all eternity for your own undoing. God washes His hands of your destruction. "What could have been done more for you that God has not done?" I take you all to witness that if I should never speak to you again, I am pure from the blood of you all. Oh barren fig trees, the Lord has been digging at your roots; and if ye bear fruit, well—if not, then ye shall be cut down.

Now I turn for a moment to you who are God's children. "I am persuaded better things of you my dearly beloved, and things that accompany salvation, though I thus speak." Yet what need there is in these trying times to search your heart and life and ask, "What fruit doth God find in me?"

What fruit of *self-abasement* is there in you? Have you found out the evil of your connection with the first Adam? Do you know the plague of your own heart, the hell of corruption that is there? Do you feel that you have never lived one moment to his glory? Do you feel that to all eternity you never can be justified by anything in yourself?

Consider often, what fruit is there *of believing* in you? Have you really and fully uptaken Christ as the Gospel lays Him down? Do you cleave to Him as a sinner? Do you count all things but loss for the excellency of the knowledge of Him? Do you feel the glory of His person, His finished work, His offices? Does

He shine like the sun into your soul? Is your heart ravished with His beauty?

Again, what fruit is there in you of crying after holiness? Is this the "one thing you do"? Do you spend your life in cries for deliverance from this body of sin and death? Ah, I fear there is little of this. Most of God's people are contented to be saved from the hell that is without; they are not so anxious to be saved from the hell that is within. I fear there is little feeling of your need of the indwelling Spirit. I fear you do not know "the exceeding greatness of His power to us-ward who believe." I fear many of you are strangers to the visits of the Comforter. God has reason to complain of you, "Wherefore should they bring forth wild grapes?"

Again, what fruit is there *of actual likeness to God* in you? Do you love to be much with God, to climb up near to God, to love and long and plead and wrestle and stretch after Him? Are you weaned from the world, from its praise, from the hatred, from the scorn? Do you give yourselves clean away to God, and all that is yours? Are you willing that your will should be lost in His great will? Do you throw yourself into the arms of God for time and for eternity? Oh, search your hearts and try them! Ask God to do it for you, and to "lead you in the way everlasting."

It fears me much that many of us may be like the fig tree by the wayside on which the hungry Saviour expected to find fruit, and He found none. Ah, we have been an ungrateful vine—minister and people. What more could God have done for us? Sunshine and shade, rain and wind, have all been given us. Goodness and severity have both been tried with us. Yet what has been returned to Him? Whether have the curses or the praises been loudest rising from our parish to heaven? Whatever does our parish more resemble—the garden of the Lord, or the howling wilderness? Whether is there more of the incense of believing prayer, or the smoke in God's nose of hypocrisy and broken sacraments?

"I write not these things to shame you, but as my beloved sons I warn you." If there be some among you—and some there are who are growing up like the lily, and bearing fruit with patience—remember, "God loveth the righteous." He that telleth the number of the stars taketh pleasure in you. Keep yourselves in the love of God. Go through again all the steps of your effectual calling. The Lord give you daily faith. Seek to have a large heart. Pray for me, that a door of utterance may be opened to me. Remember my bonds. Pray that I may utterly renounce myself, that I may be willing to do and to suffer all His will. May great grace be upon you all, now and ever more. Amen.

Dated: *Edinburgh, 27th February, 1839*

The state of the mass of unconverted souls among you has often made my heart bleed in secret.

LETTER SIX

To my dear flock, over which the Holy Ghost hath made me overseer, to all of you who are of the Church of God which He hath purchased with His own blood, your pastor wishes grace and mercy and peace.

I thank my God without ceasing that ever I was ordained over you in the Lord. For every shower of the Spirit that ever has been shed upon us, for every soul among you that has ever been added to the Church, for every disciple among you whose soul has been confirmed during our ministry, I will praise God eternally. May this letter be blessed to you by the breathing of the Holy Spirit. May it teach you and me more than ever that we are "not our own, but bought with a price."

The most striking example of self-devotedness in the cause of Christ of which I ever heard in these days of deadness was told here last week by an English minister. It has never been printed, and therefore I will relate it to you to stir up our cold hearts, that we may give our own selves unto the Lord.

The awful disease of leprosy still exists in Africa. Whether it be the very same leprosy as that mentioned in the Bible I do not know; but it is regarded as perfectly *incurable,* and so infectious that no one dares to come near. In the South of Africa there is a large Lazar-house for lepers. It is an immense space inclosed by a very high wall, and containing fields which the lepers cultivate. There is only one entrance, which is strictly guarded. Whenever any one is found with the marks of leprosy upon him, he is brought to this gate and obliged to enter in, never to return. No one is ever allowed to come out again. Within this abode of misery there are multitudes of lepers in all stages of the disease. Dr. Halbeck, a missionary of the Church of England, from the top of a neighboring hill saw them at work. He particularly noticed two sowing peas in the field. The one had no hands, the other had no feet, these members being wasted away by disease. The one who lacked hands was carrying the other who lacked feet upon his back. And he again carried in his hands the bag of seed and dropped a pea every now and then, while the other pressed it into the ground with his foot. And so they managed the work of one man between the two. Ah, how little we know of the misery that is in the world!

Such is the prison-house of disease. But you will ask, who cares for the souls of the hapless inmates? Who will venture to enter in at that dreadful gate, never to return again? Who will forsake father and mother and houses and lands to carry the message of a Saviour to these poor lepers?

Two Moravian Missionaries, impelled by a divine love for souls, have chosen the Lazar-house as their field of labor. They entered in, never to come out again. And I am told that as soon as these die, other Moravians are quite ready to fill up their place. Ah! my dear friends, may we not blush and be ashamed before God, that we—redeemed with the same blood and taught by the same Spirit—should yet be so unlike these men in vehement, heart-consuming love to Jesus and the souls of men?

I wish now to mention to you a proposal which deeply involves the happiness of you and of me, and of which I believe most of you have already heard something. Oh that you would trace the Lord's hand in it. Oh that you would "be still and know that He is God." Let me go over some of the ways by which God has led us hitherto. When I came to you at the first it was not of my seeking. I never had been in your town, and knew only one family in it. I did not ask to be made a candidate. I was quite happy where I was, laboring in the Lord's work. God turned your hearts to ask me to settle among you. It was the Lord's doing.

Since that day, "ye know after what manner I have been with you at all seasons"; and how, as far as God gave me light and strength, "I have kept back nothing that was profitable unto you, but have showed you and have taught you publicly, and from house to house." You know also, some of you in your own blessed experience, that God has given testimony to the word of His grace. It is indeed amazing that God should have blessed the word where there was so much weakness and so much sin. But "who is a God like unto our God, who forgiveth iniquity?" We planted and watered, and God gave the increase. Ye are God's husbandry. Ye are God's building. To Him be glory.

You know also that I have had some painful trials among you. The state of the mass of unconverted souls among you has often made my heart bleed in secret. The coldness and worldliness of you who are God's children has often damped me. The impossibility of fully doing the work of a minister of Christ among so many souls was a sad burden to me. The turning back of some that once cared for their souls pierced my heart with new sorrows. Still I have had two years of great joy among you—unspeakable joy—in seeing souls added to the Church of such as shall be saved. I may never be honoured to preach again, yet still to all eternity I shall praise God that He sent me to you, "For what is our hope, or joy, or crown of rejoicing? Are not even ye in the presence of our Lord Jesus Christ at His coming?"

And should I lightly break up such a connection as this? Ah no! My dear friends, I do not need all your affectionate letters to persuade me that if it were the Lord's will, my own vineyard is the happiest place for me to be. Four times other vineyards were offered to me, and I was asked to leave you; but I never for a moment listened to one of them—for ye were the seal of my ministry, and where could I be happier than where the Lord had blessed me and was still blessing me?

But God sent another message to me. He laid a heavy hand upon my body. I long struggled against it, but it was too much for me. For two months I have been an exile from you, and I have felt all the time like a widower, or like Jacob bereaved of his children. My constant prayer was that I might be restored to you and to the Lord's service. You prayed the same; and when it was not answered, I cried, "wherefore contendest Thou with me?" That word was sent in answer, "My son, despise not thou the chastening of the Lord, neither *be weary* of His correction." God seems plainly to shut the door against my returning to you at present. I am greatly better. Yet still I am forbidden to preach. I am not even allowed to conduct the family devotions morning or evening. Indeed, whenever I exert myself much in conversation, I soon feel the monitor within warning me "how frail I am."

In these circumstances the General Assembly's Committee on the Jews have this day resolved that your pastor, accompanied by Dr. Black of Aberdeen, and my beloved friend, Andrew Bonar of Collace, should travel for the next six months to make personal enquiries after the lost sheep of the house of Israel.

They propose that we should go without delay to the Holy Land, that we should then return by Smyrna, Constantinople, Poland, Germany and Holland. Now I did not seek this offer. I never dreamed of such a thing. But God suddenly threw open this door to me, while He kept the door of return to you still shut. My medical men are agreed that it is the likeliest method of restoring my broken health, and that I have strength enough for the journey. You know how my heart is engaged in the cause of Israel, and how the very sight of Immanuel's land will revive my fainting spirit. And if it be the will of God, I shall return to you, my beloved flock, to tell you all that I have seen and to lead you in the way to the Jerusalem that is above.

I cannot tell you how many providences have been sent to me, every one convincing me that it is God's will and purpose I should go. The most cheering one to me is that a young man has nearly consented to fill my place and feed your souls during my absence, who is everything I could wish. He will make you almost forget that you want your own pastor. Nay, whatever happens, I hope you will never forget me, but remember me in your families, and remember me in your secret prayers. You are all graven on my heart. I never can forget you. How wonderful have been God's dealings with us! For many reasons He has sent this affliction on us: for sin in me, for sin in you; but also, I am persuaded, that He might seek after "the dearly beloved of His soul" that are now in the hand of their enemies. His way is in the sea. His name is wonderful. I grieve to write so much about myself. I had far rather speak to you of Him Who is "fairer than the children of men." May you look beyond all ministers to Him. May He be "our guide even unto death." Once again I hope to write you before I leave my home and country. Till then, may all grace abound toward you, and peace be left on Israel. Amen.

Dated: *Edinburgh, 6 March, 1839*

Seek to be made holier every day. Pray, strive, wrestle for the Spirit to make you like God. Be as much as you can with God.

LETTER SEVEN

*To all of you who are my brethren, and my companions
in tribulation, and in the Kingdom and patience of
our Lord Jesus Christ, your pastor wishes grace and
mercy and peace.*

It gives me great joy to address you once more; and
if I could only grave in your heart some of these
words which make wise unto salvation, my time and
labor would be amply repaid.

The providences of every day convince me that I
have followed not my own will but God's in leaving
you for a time. If the Lord permit, I shall come to you
again, and I trust more fully taught by the Spirit—
a holier, happier, and more useful minister. I did not
know when I last preached to you that I was to be
so long parted from you, and thought I felt a solemn
tenderness stealing over my soul which I could not
well account for. Eternity seemed very near, and your
souls seemed very precious; yet the Lord was "leading
the blind by a way which he knew not." I have been
searching God's Word to find examples of this, and I
find there very many.

You remember Abram, how he was living quietly
in his father's house in Ur of the Chaldees when the

Lord appeared unto him and said, "Get thee out of thy country, and from thy kindred, and from thy father's house, unto a land that I will shew thee" (Gen. 12:1). "And he went out, *not knowing* whither he went." You remember Jacob. His mother said to him, "Arise, flee thou to Laban my brother to Haran; and tarry with him *a few days*" (Gen. 27:43-44). But the Lord meant it otherwise, and it was twenty years before Jacob came back again.

You remember Joseph. His father sent him a message to his brethren, "Go, I pray thee, see whether it be well with thy brethren, and well with the flocks; and bring me word again" (Gen. 37:14). He expected to see him return in a few days, but God had another purpose with him. It was more than twenty years before he saw the face of Joseph again, till he said, "It is enough; Joseph my son is yet alive: I will go and see him before I die" (Gen. 45:28).

You will find the same method of dealing in the New Testament. How little Peter knew that morning when he went up to the housetop to pray that he was that very day to be sent away to open the door of faith to the Gentiles. And yet God said to him, "Arise therefore, and get thee down, and go with them, *doubting nothing*" (Acts 10:20).

Again, you remember how happily Barnabas and Saul were engaged with the brethren at Antioch, ministering to the Lord and fasting. Little did they think that the next day they would be sailing away to carry the Gospel to other lands. "As they ministered to the Lord, and fasted, the Holy Ghost said, Separate Me Barnabas and Saul for the work whereunto I have called them. And when they had fasted and prayed, and laid their hands on them, they sent them away" (Acts 13:2-3).

Once more, when Paul had preached the Gospel in all the cities of Asia, and was now come to Troas on the sea coast, how little did he think that night when he laid his head upon his pillow that by the next morning he would be sailing away to carry the message of salvation to another continent! "A vision appeared to Paul in the night. There stood a man of Macedonia, and prayed him, saying, Come over into Macedonia, and help us. And. . . immediately we endeavoured to go into Macedonia, assuredly gathering that the Lord had called us for to preach the gospel unto them" (Acts 16:9-10).

Now has not God dealt with us in a similar manner? Although we are nothing in ourselves but vile and hell-deserving creatures, yet when accepted in the beloved, God cares for us. Oh, we "err, not knowing the Scriptures, nor the power of God," when we think that God is indifferent to the least of all that are in Christ. We are fastened on the Redeemer's shoulder. We are graven on His breastplate, and that is on the Redeemer's heart. Surely He hath directed our steps.

Oh the depth of the riches both of the wisdom and the knowledge of God! In other circumstances, I suppose I would not have listened to this proposal. I could not have torn myself away, had I been in strength and usefulness among you. And indeed, the expedition would probably never have been thought of. But God, Who chose Israel to be His peculiar treasure, can easily open up ways when His set time is come. I parted from you only for a few days; but God meant otherwise, and He will make it His own fixed time.

"And now, behold, I know that there are some of you, among whom I have gone preaching the kingdom of God, who shall see my face no more." He that keepeth Israel may preserve your pastor under His almighty feathers. I know you will pray for me as you have done in secret and in your families and in your meetings for prayer, "that the sun may not hurt me by day, nor the moon by night." But if I should come back again, will I find you all where I left you? Alas, I know it cannot be so. For "what is your life? It is even a vapour." And God is still crying, "Return, ye children of men."

For some among you, "I give thanks unto the Father, that He hath made you meet to be partakers of the inheritance of the saints in light." There are some among you from whom I have learned more than I taught you. You have been "succourers of many, and of myself also," and have often reminded me of corn when it is fully ripe. Should we be surprised if God puts in the sickle? Dear advanced believers, we may never meet again. I feel it almost wrong to pray that you may be kept to comfort us on our return. It is wrong to grudge you an entrance into "perfect day," where you will lay aside that body of death and sin which is your greatest grief. Yet may the Lord spare you, and bless you, and make you a blessing, that you may bear fruit in old age. Oh, fill up the little inch of time that remains to His glory. Walk with God. Live for God. Oh that every thought and work and action might be in His favour and to His praise. The Lord grant that we may meet where we shall "walk with Christ in white." God Who knows my heart knows it would be hell to me to spend an eternity with unconverted, Christless souls. But to be with Christ and His people is Heaven to me where it is.

There are many young believers among you whom I may never meet again. It is hard to think of parting with you. The mother feels it hard to part with the sucking child. So it is my highest delight in this world to see you growing day by day, to see your sense of the plague of your own heart deepening, to see you "cleaving to Christ with full purpose of heart," to see your peace widening like a river, and to see your love burning higher and higher toward the throne of God. You are in my heart to live and to die with me. Still, He Who at any time fed you by me can as easily feed you by another. I "commend you to the Lord on Whom you believe." Read 2 Peter 3:17. Meditate over it. Pray over it. "Beware lest ye also, being led away with the error of the wicked, fall from your own steadfastness. But grow in grace." The only way to be kept from falling is *"to grow."* If you stand still you will fall. Read Proverbs 11:28. "The righteous shall *flourish as a branch."* Remember, you are not a tree which can stand alone, you are only "a branch." And it is only while you abide in Him as a branch that you will flourish. Keep clear your sense of justification. Remember it is not your own natural goodness, nor your tears, nor your sanctification that will justify you before God. It is Christ's sufferings and obedience alone.

Seek to be made holier every day. Pray, strive, wrestle for the Spirit to make you like God. Be as much as you can with God. I declare to you that I had rather be one hour with God than a thousand with the sweetest society on earth or in heaven. All other joys are but streams—God is the fountain. "All my springs are in Thee." Now may the blessings that are on the head of the just be on your head. Be faithful unto death, and Christ will give you a crown of life. And if I never meet you again in this world, may I meet you as pillars in the house of my God, where you shall "go no more out." Pray for me when you have access to the throne, when you have a heart for it. I will try to pray for you, that you may endure to the end.

I have a word for those of you that are still uncon- verted, whom I may never see again in the flesh. My heart bleeds to think of parting with you. But I must defer this to my next letter, for I expect to write you again before I go. Farewell for the present, and may the grace of the Lord Jesus Christ be with your spirits.

Dated: *Edinburgh, 13th March, 1839*

Dear Christians, I often think it strange that ever we shall be in heaven, and so many in hell through our soul-destroying carelessness.

LETTER EIGHT

*To all of you, my dear flock, who are dearly beloved
and longed for, my joy and crown, your pastor wishes
grace and mercy and peace from God our Father and
our Lord Jesus Christ.*

In my last letter I showed you that in all human
probability there are many of you to whom I have
preached the blessed Gospel of salvation to whom I
shall never preach it again face to face. I cannot be
blind to the many dangers that accompany foreign
travel—the diseases and accidents to which we shall
be exposed. But if through your prayer I be given
to you again, how many blanks I shall find in my
flock—how many dear children of God gone to be
where the weary are at rest, where the imperfect are
"made perfect"? How many of you that have stood
out against all the invitations of Christ and all the
warnings of God shall I find departed to give in your
account before the throne? It is to these last I wish
now to speak. For two years I have testified to you the
Gospel of the grace of God. I came to you "in weakness, and in fear, and in much trembling." And if the
case of the children of God and of backsliding souls
has often lain heavy at my heart, I can truly say that

your dreadful condition—"settled like wine upon its lees," when you are about to be "turned upside down as a man turneth a dish and wipeth it"—has been a continual anxiety to me; and sometimes, when I have had glimpses of the reality of eternal things, it has been an insupportable agony to my spirit. I know well that this is a jest to you; that you care not whether ministers go or stay; and if you get a short enough sermon on the Sabbath day that will soothe and not prick your conscience, that is all you care for. Still, it may be that the Lord Who opened Manasseh's heart will open yours while I go over solemnly, in the sight of God, what appear to be the chief reasons why, after my two years' ministry among you, there are still so many unconverted, perishing souls.

One cause is to be sought in your minister. In Malachi 2:6 you will find a sweet description of a faithful and successful minister: "The law of truth was in his mouth, and iniquity was not found in his lips: he walked with me in peace and equity, and did turn many away from iniquity." This is what we should have been. But the furnace brings out the dross, and afflictions discover defects unknown before. Oh that I could say with Paul, that "I have been with you at all seasons, serving the Lord with all humility of mind, and with many tears." "Ye are witnesses, and God also, how holily and justly and unblameably we behaved ourselves among you that believe." I am indeed amazed that the ministry of such a worm as I am should ever have been blessed among you at all; and I do this day bewail before you every sin in my heart and life that has kept back the light from your poor dark souls. Oh, you that can pray, pray that I may come back a holy minister, a shepherd to lead the flock not by the voice only, but to walk before them in the way of life.

Looking back over my pulpit work, alas! I see innumerable deficiencies. I always prayed that I might "not keep back anything that was profitable"; that I might "not shun to declare the whole counsel of God"; that "I might decrease and Christ increase." Still also, alas! how dimly I have seen and set before you "the truth as it is in Jesus." How coldly have I pleaded with you to "save yourselves from this untoward generation." How many things I have known among you "beside Christ and Him crucified." How often I have preached myself and not the Saviour. How little I have "expounded to you in all the Scriptures the things concerning Jesus."

One error more has been in my private labors among you. How much fruitless conversation I have had with you. I have not been like a shepherd crying after the lost sheep, nor like a physician among dying men, nor like a servant bidding you to the marriage, nor like one plucking brands out of the burning. How often have I gone to your houses to try to win your souls, and you have put me off with a little worldly talk, and the words of salvation have died upon my lips. I dared not tell you you were perishing. I dared not to show you plainly of the Saviour. How often I have sat at some of your tables and my heart yearned for your souls, yet a false shame kept me silent. How often I have gone home saying bitterly, "free me from blood guiltiness, O God, Thou God of my salvation."

I turn now to the causes in you dear children of God. You also have hindered, in great measure, God's work in the parish.

1. *By your lack of holiness.* "Ye are the light of the world." I have often told you that a work of revival in any place almost always begins with the children of God. God pours water first on "him that is thirsty," and then on "the dry ground." But ah, how little has "the Word of the Lord sounded out from you"! I do not mean that you should have been loud talkers about religious things; "in the multitude of words there wanteth not sin"; and "the talk of the lips tendeth to penury." But oh, you should have been "living epistles, known and read of all men." You know a lighted lamp is a very small thing, and it burns calmly and without noise, yet "it gives light to all that are in the house." So if you had had day by day the blood of Christ upon your conscience, walking as a forgiven and adopted child of God, having a calm peace in your bosom, and

a heavenly hope in your eye, having the Holy Spirit filling you with a sweet, tender, chaste, compassionate, forgiving love to all the world; oh, had you shone thus for two years back, how many of your friends and neighbors that are going down to hell might have been saying this day, "Thy people shall be my people, and thy God my God." Think, my beloved friends, that every act of unholiness, of conformity to the world, of selfishness, of whispering and backbiting, is hindering the work of God in the parish, and ruining souls eternally. Ah! what shall I say to those of you who, instead of emitting the sweet, winning light of holiness, have given out only rays of darkness? "I have this against thee, that thou hast left thy first love. Remember therefore from whence thou art fallen, and repent, and do the first works; or else I will come unto thee quickly, and will remove thy candlestick out of his place, except thou repent" (Rev. 2:4-5).

2. *You have hindered God's work by your lack of prayer.* When God gives grace to souls, it is in answer to the prayers of His children. You will see this on the day of Pentecost (Acts 2). Ezekiel 37:9 shows that in answer to the prayer of a single child of God, God will give grace to a whole valley full of dry and prayerless bones. When God puts it into the heart of His children to pray, it is certain that He is going to pour down His Spirit in abundance. Now where have been your prayers, oh children of God? The salvation of

those around you depends on your asking, and yet "hitherto have ye asked nothing in Christ's name." "Ye that are the Lord's remembrancers, keep not silence, and give Him no rest." Alas, you have given God much rest. You have allowed His hand to remain unplucked out of His bosom. It is said of John Welsh, minister of Ayr, that he used always to sleep with a plaid upon his bed, that he might wrap it round him when he rose in the night to pray. He used to spend whole nights in wrestling with God for Zion, and for the purity of the Church of Scotland, and he wondered how Christians could lie all night in bed without rising to pray. Ah! we have few Welshes now; therefore our Church is so dim, and our land a barren wilderness.

Dear Christians, I often think it strange that ever we shall be in heaven, and so many in hell through our soul-destroying carelessness. The good Lord pardon the past, and stir you up for the future. I learn that you are more stirred up to pray since I left, both in secret and unitedly. God grant it be so. Continue in it, dear children. Do not let it slip again. Plead and wrestle with God, showing Him that the cause is *His Own,* and that it is all for *His Own* glory to arise and have mercy upon Zion.

Last of all, think on the causes in yourselves, oh unconverted souls. Be sure of this, that you will only have yourselves to blame if you awake in hell. You will not be able to plead God's secret decrees, nor the sins of your minister, nor the carelessness of your godly neighbors. You will be speechless. If you die, it is because you will die; and if you will die, then you must die.

Think:

1. *On your carelessness about ordinances.* They are the channels through which God pours His Spirit. The Bible, prayer, the house of God—these are the golden pipes through which the golden oil is poured. How many of you utterly neglect the Bible? You know not the blessedness of the man spoken of in the 1st Psalm. How many of you restrain prayer before God? How many of you have dead, useless prayers learned by rote? And oh, how you despise the house of God. Alas, that church shall rise against you in judgment! It was a door of the ark brought near to you. Two years and more the gates have been wide open for you, and yet how you have slighted it. Already I seem to hear your loud wailing, "when you mourn at the last. . . and say, How have I hated instruction, and my heart despised reproof, and have not obeyed the voice of my teachers!"

2. *Think how you have been mockers.* It has been too common for you to make a mock of eternal things and of godly people. When there have been anxious souls seeking the way to be saved, and they could not

conceal their tears, you have called them hypocrites! When some have got a new heart and have changed their way of life, you have spoken scoffingly of them and tried to bring them into contempt. Alas, poor soul, look within! You have hardened your own heart into an adamant stone. Look at Proverbs 17:5, "He that mocketh the poor reproacheth His maker." And again, Isaiah 28:22, "Now therefore be ye not *mockers, lest your bands be made strong.*"

3. To sum up all: *The great cause that I leave you hardened is that you despise the Son of God.* You see no beauty in Him that you should desire Him. You lightly esteem the Rock of your salvation. You have not had a soul-piercing look at a pierced Saviour. You have not seen the infinite load of sins that weighed down His blessed head. You have not seen how open His arms are to receive you—how often He would have gathered you. You have not heard that sweet whisper of the Spirit, "Behold Me, Behold Me," which, when a man once hears, he leaves all and follows. You have trampled under foot the blood of the Son of God.

Farewell dear, dear souls. God knows that my whole heart prays that you may be saved. Perhaps there are some of you that never would bend under my ministry that will melt like wax before the fire under the word of the dear young minister who is to speak to you in my absence. May the Lord give him hundreds for my tens. I will often pray for you, and sometimes write to you, when I am far away. If I reach Immanuel's land, I will say, "The Lord bless you out of Zion." And if you will not turn, remember I take God for a record that I am pure from the blood of you all.

Dear children of God, I now cast you on Him Who cast you on me. When I was ordained over you, He said to me, "Feed My sheep; feed My lambs; tend My sheep." Now, when He sends me away, I would humbly return His own words to Him, saying, "Oh Shepherd of Israel, feed my sheep; feed my lambs; tend my sheep."

Little children, love one another. Keep yourselves from idols. Bear me ever on your hearts. Pray that when I have preached to others, I may not be a castaway. Pray that I may save some. Now the God of peace, that brought again from the dead our Lord Jesus, that great Shepherd of the sheep, through the blood of the everlasting covenant, make you perfect in every good work to do His will, working in you that which is well pleasing in His sight through Jesus Christ. To Whom be glory for ever and ever. Amen. (My next, if God will, may be from England.)

Dated: *Edinburgh, 20 March, 1839*

Do you really delight in the Sabbath day? If not, you are no child of God.

LETTER NINE

To all of you, my beloved flock, who have received Christ and walk in Him, your pastor wishes grace, mercy and peace from God our Father, and from our Lord Jesus Christ.

My heart's desire and prayer for you every day is that you may be saved. I am now far from you in the flesh, yet am I with you in the Spirit. I thank my God without ceasing for the many of you who have been awakened to flee from the wrath to come, who have rested your souls upon the good word of God concerning Jesus, and who have tasted the love of God. In every prayer of mine for you all I ask that you may continue in the faith, grounded and settled, that you may be live trees rooted in Christ Jesus, or like a holy temple built up in Him Who is the only foundation stone.

I expected to have written you from London, and again before leaving France; but we have travelled so rapidly—often day and night—and the fatigue was so great to my weak frame that I was disappointed in this. But I did not forget you night or day, and I know well I am not forgotten by you. Since I wrote you last, I have passed through many cities and countries and seen many faces and things strange to me. Many lessons for my own soul and for yours I have learned. At present I must write you briefly.

We left London on the 11th of April, and the next morning crossed the British Channel from Dover to Boulogne and found ourselves on the shores of France. The very first night we spent in France we were visited by a most interesting Jew, evidently anxious about his soul. He spoke with us for many hours, accepted the New Testament in Hebrew, and bade us goodbye with much emotion. We thanked God for this token for good. Pray for us that God may give us good success, that we may have the souls of Israel for our hire.

From Boulogne we travelled to Paris a day and a night and spent Sabbath there. Alas, poor Paris knows no Sabbath. All the shops are open, and all the inhabitants are on the wing in search of pleasures—pleasures that perish in the using. I thought of Babylon and of Sodom as I passed through the crowd. You cannot tell how I longed for the peace of a Scottish Sabbath. There is a place in Paris called the Chauns Elysees—or "Plain of Heaven"—a beautiful public walk with trees and gardens. We had to cross it in going to the Protestant chapel. It is the chief scene of their Sabbath desecration, and an awful scene it is. Ah, thought I, if this is the heaven a Parisian loves, he will never enjoy the pure heaven that is above. Try yourselves by that text, Isaiah 58:13-14. I remember once preaching to you from it. Do you really delight in the Sabbath day? If not, you are no child of God. I remember with grief that there are many among you that despise the Sabbath; some that buy and sell on that holy day; some who spend its blessed hours in worldly pleasure, in folly and sin. Ah, you would make Dundee another Paris if you could. Dear believers, oppose these ungodly practises with all your might. The more that others dishonor God's holy day, the more do you honor it and show that you love it of all the seven the best. Even in Paris, as in Sardis, we found a little flock of believers. We heard a sweet sermon in English, and another in French. There are only two thousand Protestant hearers out of the half million that inhabit Paris, and there are fourteen faithful sermons preached every Sabbath day.

We left the French capital on 16th April, a lovely evening with a deep blue sky above and a lovely country before us on the banks of the Seine. This would be a delightsome land if only it had the light of God's countenance upon it. We travelled three days and three nights by Troyes, Dijon, and Chalous, till we came to Lyons upon the rapid river Rhone in the South of France. The Lord stirred up kind friends to meet us. Lyons is famous as being the place where many Christians were martyred in the first ages, and where many were burned at the time of the Reformation because they loved and confessed the Lord Jesus.

God loves the place still. There is a small body of three hundred believers who live here under a faithful pastor, M. Cordees. He cheered our hearts much and sent us away with affectionate prayers. Next day we sailed down the Rhone more than a hundred miles through a most wonderful country. We hoped to have spent the Sabbath at Marseilles; but just as we entered the Mediterranean sea, a storm of wind arose and drove the vessel on a barren island at the mouth of the Rhone. We all landed and spent our Sabbath quietly on the desert island. It was your Communion Sabbath, and I thought perhaps this providence was given me that I might have a quiet day to pray for you.

There were about twelve fishermen's huts on the island, made of reeds, with a vine growing before the door and a fig tree in their garden. We gave tracts and books in French to all our fellow passengers and to the inhabitants, and tried to hallow the Sabbath. My heart went up to God the whole day for you all, and for my dear friends who would be ministering to you. I tried to go over you one by one, as many as I could call to mind. My longing desire for you was that Jesus might reveal Himself to you in the breaking of bread, that you might have heart-filling views of the lovely person of Immanuel, and might draw from Him rivers of comfort, life and holiness. I trust your fellowship was with the Father and with His Son Jesus Christ. Many, I know, are ignorant of Jesus. I trembled when I thought of their taking the bread and wine. You know all my mind upon this.

The next morning the storm abated. We sailed over the tideless sea and reached the beautiful harbor of Marseilles by 8 o'clock. We had conference with a faithful young minister, and with the Rabbi of the Jews. We also attended the Synagogue the same evening. The Jews of France are fast falling into infidelity, especially the younger Jews. They do not love the law and the prophets as their fathers did. They are indeed the dry bones in Ezekiel 37. Still, God can make them live. It is our part to speak to them the word of the Lord and to pray for the quickening Spirit.

True Christians in France are increasing. There are four hundred Protestant ministers, and nearly one half of these are faithful men who know nothing among their flocks but Christ and Him crucified. In some places Christians seem much more bold and devoted than in Scotland. It is very pleasant to hear them singing the French Psalms—they sing with all their heart—and they are much given to prayer. Oh my dear Christians, be like them in these things. May the same Holy Spirit Who has often visited you in times gone by fill your hearts more than ever with praises and prayer.

Popery in France is waxing bolder. The first day we landed on the shore it was evident we were in a land of popish darkness. On the height above Boulogne, a tall white cross attracted our eyes. We found on it an image of the Saviour nailed to the tree—larger than life—the spear, the hammer, the nails, the sponge were all there. It was raised by some shipwrecked fishermen, and sailor's wives go there in a storm to pray for their absent husbands.

The popish priests meet us in every street. They wear a three-cornered hat, black bands, a black mantle with a sash, and large buckles in their shoes. They have all a dark, suspicious look about them. At the entrance of every village there is a cross, and the churches are full of pictures and images. I went into one church in Paris, the finest in France, where the crosses were all of pure silver, and there was a large white image of the Virgin Mary holding the infant Jesus in her arms. Many rich and poor were kneeling on the pavement before the image, silently praying. Gross darkness covers the people.

A priest travelled one whole night with us in the coach. We argued with him first in French and then in Latin, trying to convince him of his errors, showing him his need of peace with God and a new heart. In the 137th Psalm you will see that Babylon, or Popery, is "doomed to destruction"; and in Revelation 18 you will see that her destruction will be very sudden and very terrible. Oh that it may soon come, for thousands are perishing under its soul-destroying errors! And yet, remember what I used to read to you out of Martin

Boos, and remember the saying of the Lord to Elijah (1 Kings 19). There may be many hidden ones even in Babylon. The whole way through France we distributed French tracts. Many hundreds in this way received a message of life. In every village they came crowding round us to receive them. Pray that the dew of the Spirit may make the seed sown by the wayside spring up.

We were too late for the first vessel to Malta, and therefore resolved to sail into Italy. We left Marseilles on the 23rd of April and landed in Genoa on the 24th. Genoa is one of the most beautiful towns in the world. Most of the houses and churches are of pure white marble, and from the sea look like palaces; but Satan's seat is there. We dared not distribute a single tract or book in Genoa. We would have been imprisoned immediately. The Catholic priests in their black, dismal cloaks, and the monks with their coarse brown dress tied with a cord, a crucifix, and beads hanging round their neck, bare feet, and cowl, swarm in every street. I counted that we met twenty of them in a ten minutes walk. Popery reigns here triumphant; yet the people are sitting still and at ease, living for this world only. Oh, it is an awful thing to be at ease when under the wrath of God! Every place I see in Italy makes me praise God that you have the Gospel so freely preached unto you. Oh prize it highly. Do not neglect the wells of salvation that flow so freely for you.

The next day we sailed for Leghorn, where we have been ever since. We are living in the house where the excellent Mr. Martin, once minister of St. George's, Edinburgh, died in 1834. We visited his grave. I prayed that, like him, we might be faithful even unto death. There are from 10,000 to 20,000 Jews here. We went to the synagogue the night we arrived, and twice since. It is a beautiful building inside, capable of holding 2000 persons. The place where they keep the Law written on a parchment roll is finely ornamented with marble; so is the desk where they read the prayers. Lamps are kept continually burning. One Rabbi was chanting the prayers when we entered. Beside the ark there stood three Rabbis in the Eastern dress, with turbans and flowing robes and long beards. They were much revered, and many came to kiss their hand and receive their blessing. One of them is from Jerusalem. We have had many interesting conversations with him. Every day we have met with several Jews. They are very friendly to us, and we try to convince them out of the Scriptures that Jesus is the Christ. There are about 250 Protestants here, and we have tried to stir them up also to care for their souls. Dr. Black preached to them in our Hotel last Sabbath evening.

Hitherto the Lord hath helped us. Tomorrow we sail from Italy for Malta, then for Egypt, and then for the Holy Land. Dear believers, it is a sweet consolation to me that your prayers go with me wherever I go. Often, perhaps, they close the mouth of the adversary—often keep back the storms from our vessel—often open a way to the hearts of those we meet—often bring down a sweet stream of the Spirit to water my thirsty soul. May I be enabled to make a sweet exchange with you, praying my heavenly Father to render double into each of your bosoms what you pray for me. May my dear brother, who I trust fills my place among you, be made a blessing to you all. May his own soul be watered while he waters yours. Join him with me in your supplications. May he turn many souls among you that I could never turn. This is Thursday evening. I trust you are at this moment met together in the prayer meeting. Oh, do not forsake the assembling of yourselves together. My heart is with you all. May the Spirit fill the whole church and every heart with His presence and power.

My body is still far from being strong. I am more and more convinced that I did right in leaving you. I trust to be restored to you again in the fullness of the blessing of the Gospel of Christ. "The will of the Lord be done." My dear brother who is with me, whom you know well, and who daily joins me in fervent prayers for you, sends his salutation. Remember me to all who are sick and afflicted. Alas, how many of you may be laboring and heavy laden that I know not of. But Jesus knows your sorrows. I commend you to the good Physician.

My dear classes I do not and cannot forget. I pray that Psalm 119:9 may be written in your hearts. My dear children in the Sabbath Schools I always think upon on the Sabbath evenings, and on those who patiently labor among them. The Lord Himself give you encouragement and a full reward. To all I say, keep close to Christ, dear friends. Do not be enticed away from Him. He is all your righteousness and all mine. Out of Him you have all your strength and I mine. "It pleased the Father that in Him should all fulness dwell." The grace of the Lord Jesus Christ be with your spirits. Farewell.

Dated: *Leghorn, 2 May, 1839*

See that no fleshly lust, no covetousness, which is idolatry, no hankering after the world and its unholy pleasures, no unlawful affection, be reigning in you.

LETTER TEN

To my dear flock whom I love in the Lord, grace, mercy and peace be multiplied from God the Father, and from His Son, Jesus Christ.

I fear that many of you will be thinking hardly of your distant pastor because of his long silence, and indeed I cannot but think hardly of myself. I little thought when leaving Italy that I would be in Europe again before writing to you. I did not know how difficult it is to write at any length when travelling in the East. From the day we left Egypt till we came to Lebanon, for more than two months we were constantly journeying from place to place, living in tents, without the luxury of a chair or a bed. In these circumstances, with my weak body, and under a burning sun, you must not wonder at my silence.

At the foot of Mount Carmel I began one letter to you. Once again, in sight of the sea of Galilee I began another; but neither did I get finished. Last of all, before leaving the Holy Land I set apart a day for writing to you; but God had another lesson for me to learn. He laid me down under a burning fever, bringing me to the very gates of death. Indeed, my dear people, I feel like Lazarus, whom the Lord Jesus raised from the tomb. I feel like one sent a second time with the message of salvation to speak it more feelingly and more faithfully to your hearts, as one whose eye has looked into an eternal world. In all our wanderings you have been with me by night and by day. Every scene of Immanuel's land brought you to my remembrance, because every scene tells of Jesus Christ and Him crucified. In the wilderness, in Jerusalem, beside the Sea of Galilee, at Smyrna, on the Black Sea, on the Danube—you have been all with me. I have day and night unceasingly laid your case before God. It has been one of my chief comforts that, though I could not preach to you nor come to you, I could yet pray for you. Perhaps I may obtain more for you in this way than I could have done by my personal services among you.

Another joy to me has been that I know all of you that pray, pray for me. This has been a lamp to me in many a dark hour. God has wonderfully preserved us through your prayers. In the south of the Holy Land we were daily exposed to the plague. Every night we heard the wail of the mourners going about the streets of Jerusalem. Yet no plague came near our dwelling. Near the Sea of Galilee we were often in danger of being robbed and murdered by the wild Arabs, yet we passed unhurt through the midst of them. Sailing to Smyrna, your pastor was brought low indeed, insomuch that I never thought to see you again; yet

He sent His word and healed me. In Poland, the Sabbath before last, I was actually in the hands of robbers; but through God's wonderful mercy I escaped safe. In every step of our journey, I am persuaded we have been watched over by an all loving Father Who is the hearer of prayer. And the Lord shall deliver us from every evil work, and will preserve us unto His heavenly Kingdom. I speak of these things only that you may give Him the glory and trust Him to your dying day. Sing the 116th Psalm in all your families.

Another joy to me has been that God has given you my dear brother, who watches over you so tenderly. You know not what joy it gave me to hear of you all through him. The letter reached me at Smyrna, when I was so weak that I could not walk alone. It was like health and marrow to my bones to hear that the Lord's work is not yet done in the midst of you, and that so many of you stand fast in the Lord, having your conversation in heaven. I have no greater joy than to hear that my children walk in the truth. It is not like common joy. All joys of this world are short and fading, they reach not beyond the dark boundary of the grave. But to rejoice over those whom the Lord has given us out of a perishing world, this is a joy which God Himself shares and which reaches into the light of eternity. You are my joy and crown. In like manner, there is no sorrow like the sorrow of the pastor who has to weep over a backsliding people. I do tremble to return to you, for I know well I shall have deep sorrow from some of whom I expected joy. I fear lest I have to mourn over some branches that are without fruit on the good vine tree—over some who once gave their hand to the Saviour, but are now saying, "I will go after my lovers." Oh, are there none of you have left your first love, and broken the bands that bound you to follow Jesus? Shall I find none of whom I must needs say, "They went out from us, but they were not of us"? Oh, there is no sorrow like unto this sorrow.

Had I been able, as I hoped, to have written you from all the chief places in our journeyings, I would have attempted to describe to you all I saw. But now there are so many countries to look back upon that it would be vain to attempt it. I do hope that if the Lord brings us together again I may be able to tell you many things of our wanderings, and especially of Immanuel's land, which may both refresh and improve you. Nothing that I have would I keep back from you if only it be for your soul's good and our Lord's glory.

Of the Holy Land I can only say like the Queen of Sheba, that the half was not told me. It is far more wonderful than I could have believed. I shall always reckon it one of the greatest temporal blessings of my lot that I have been led to wander over its mountains with the Bible in my hand, to sit by its wells, and to meditate among its ruined cities. Not a single day did we spend there without reading in the land itself the most wonderful traces of God's anger and of His love. Several times we went to the Mount of Olives, to the garden of Gethsemane, to the pool of Siloam, and to the village of Bethany; and every stone seemed to speak of the love of God to sinners. These places are probably very little altered from what they were in the days when Jesus tabernacled among men. And they all seemed to say, "Hereby perceive we the love of God, because He laid down His life for us." We were four days in sight of the Sea of Galilee. I could not help thinking of you, my dear young people, for we used to go over the Sea of Galilee so often on the Monday evenings, and all the scenes of divine love it has been witness to.

One day we rode through the plain of Gennesareth and passed the moldering ruins of Capernaum—the Saviour's city—where His voice of mercy was so often heard, and where His hand was so often stretched out to heal. We asked in vain for Chorazin and Bethsaida—the woe which Jesus pronounced has fallen upon them. Oh my dear flock, how shall you escape if you neglect so great a salvation? See how desolate they are left who refuse Him that speaketh from heaven. The free offer of a divine Surety rings through your churches now. God continues faithful teachers among you. Every Sabbath and oftener the fountain for sin is publicly opened for you, and souls all-defiled with sin are invited to come and wash. But these mercies will not always last. If you tread the glorious Gospel of the grace of God under your feet, your soul will perish, and I fear Dundee will one day be a howling wilderness like Capernaum.

I spent nearly the whole of August during my illness in Bouja, a village near Smyrna, under the care of tenderest friends whom the Lord wonderfully prepared for me in a strange land. You remember Smyrna is one of the seven Churches of Asia to which the Saviour sent those quickening messages in the Revelation of John. I thought again and again of the happy Thursday evenings which I once spent with you in meditating on these seven epistles to the Churches. You know it was said of Samuel, even when he was a child, that "God did let none of his words fall to the ground." And the same is true this hour of the very weakest of God's faithful ministers. What we have spoken to you is not like the passing wind which hurries on and leaves no trace behind. It is like the rain and snow. It will not return to God without accomplishing some end in your hearts, either melting or hardening.

Smyrna is the only one of these Churches where a pure golden candlestick is now to be found with the light burning. There is a small company who believe in Jesus. It was pleasant indeed to hear the Gospel preached there in all its purity and power. Be you also faithful to death, and you shall receive a crown of life.

Leaving Smyrna, we sailed past Troas and Bithynia and visited Constantinople—the most beautiful city in the world and yet the most miserable. Looking round from the deck of the vessel I could count above ninety minarets, many of pure marble, carved and gilded in the richest manner. These all form parts of Mosques or temples of the false prophet Mahomet. His religion is a singular invention of Satan. Their Koran or Bible is a book filled with nonsense and with much wickedness. All their belief is comprehended in the short saying, "Sa Ullah il Ullah UMahommed Rasul Ullah"—"There is no God but Allah, and Mohammed is his prophet." They expect to be saved chiefly by making pilgrimages to Mecca and Jerusalem, by abstaining from wine and pork, and by praying four times a day. Every day at sunrise or sunset we saw them at prayer. Wherever they are—on the open street, on top of the house, or on the deck of a ship—they take off their shoes, wash their hands, face and feet, spread their garment before them, turn their face toward Mecca, and then pray, bending and kissing the ground often fifteen and twenty times. They are rather pleased if you look at them. They are very proud of their own faith, and will not listen for a moment to the Gospel of Jesus. It would be instant punishment or death if any missionary were to attempt their conversion.

Ah, my dear flock, how differently you are situated! How freely salvation is offered to you—a faith that really saves you from your sins, that makes you love one another—for love is of God, and every one that loveth is born of God. If you are not growing humble and loving, be sure your faith is no better than a Mahometan's. You are not of God but of the world.

The next countries we visited were Wallachia and Moldavia. We sailed to them from Constantinople, across the raging waves of the Black Sea and up the mighty river Danube. These are two similar countries, seldom visited by travellers. They are governed by two princes, and the established religion is that of the Greek Church. I wish I could show you all that I have seen of the superstition and wickedness practised among them, that you might give more earnest heed to the pure Gospel that flows as freely as air and water through our beloved land.

One day in Bucharest, the capital city of Wallachia, I was present at a festival on the Prince's birthday. An immense crowd was present in their finest church, and all the nobles of the land. The service consisted of prayers and chanting by a number of priests dressed in the most splendid manner. When all was over, I stayed behind to see a curious superstition. At one side of the altar lay an open coffin, highly ornamented. Within I observed a dead body, wrapped in cloth of gold. A dead, shrivelled hand was left out. This is said to be the body of Saint Demetrius, later found in a river, by the waters parting asunder miraculously. Such is the tale we were told. I stood beside it while the worshippers approached the coffin in great numbers, men and women, rich and poor. First they crossed themselves and kneeled, kissing the floor three times. Then they approached reverently and kissed the withered hand of the dead body and of the cross that lay beside it. Then they gently dropped a small coin into a little plate at the dead man's feet, and after receiving a blessing from the priest, with three prostrations more to the ground, they retired. This is one specimen of their abominable worship of dead men.

Do I tell you these things that you may be proud of your superior light? Ah no. I write these things that those of you who live no better lives than they do may be convinced of your danger. What can you expect of these poor idolaters but that they will live after the flesh in rioting and drunkenness—in chambering and wantonness—in strife and envying? But are there none of you, my dear flock, for whom night and day my prayers ascend—are there none of you who do the same things? Though you have the Holy Bible, and a freely preached Gospel, and no superstitions, yet how many of you live an unholy life? Ah, remember Sardis: "I know thy works, that thou hast a name that thou livest, and art dead. Be watchful, and strengthen the things which remain, that are ready to die: for I have not found thy works perfect before God."

The next kingdom we came through was Austrian Poland, the land of graven images. We came through the chief cities—Tarnapole, Brody, Lemberg—and from there to Cracow, travelling many hundred miles. You would be amazed, as I have been, if you saw the abominable idolatry of this land. The Roman Catholic is the established faith, and the government are bitter persecutors of any who change. At every village there are numbers of crosses of immense size with the image of the Saviour. There are also statues of the Virgin Mary, and of other saints—as large as life—all along the roads. Often there are wooden boxes set up full of images. Often in the middle of a square there is a small covered chamber full of these idols of wood and stone, where the poor people worship every day.

The Bible is an unlawful book in this country. All our Bibles were taken away from us—even our Hebrew ones—that we might not preach to the Jews the glad tidings of a Saviour. Blessed be God, they could not take them from our memories and hearts. Should not this make you all pray for the coming of the day when the towers of Popery shall fall, the day when God shall avenge us on her? For the Bible, which she hates so much, says, "Her plagues shall come in one day, death, and mourning, and famine; and she shall be utterly burned with fire: for strong is the Lord

God Who judgeth her." Pray for that day, for it will be the same day when God will bind up the breach of His people Israel, and shall heal the stroke of their wound. It will be the day when the Lamb's wife shall come forth in all her loveliness, and when the Lord Jesus shall wear the crown of His espousals.

I began this letter to you in Cracow, the ancient capital of Poland, but now an independent state. We spent three days there, enquiring after the poor, despised Jews. We had much fellowship with a faithful, prayerful missionary who labors among them there; and on the Sabbath we celebrated the Lord's supper. During the four years he has been in Cracow, the missionary had never once enjoyed the ordinance, for all around are sunk in Popery or infidelity. We were but five souls in all; and yet we felt it very pleasant, when surrounded with them that hate us, and far from our houses, with the door of the chamber shut, to remember Jesus. My thoughts and desires were much toward you. I had greatly hoped to be present at your next Lord's supper, but now I see it cannot be. My only comfort is that I have committed you to those who are beloved in the Lord, workmen that need not to be ashamed, whose names are in the Book of life. And the Chief Shepherd, I feel persuaded, will not leave you orphans, but will come to you and breathe upon you. May the Lord keep back from the table all who are not united to Christ, and may you who are

His own children have communion with the Father and with his Son, Jesus Christ.

Since yesterday morning we have travelled 180 miles nearer home. We are now in Breslau, and we breathe more freely, for this is the Protestant Kingdom of Prussia. It makes my heart light to think that I am really on my way to you. It has been a sweet work to me indeed to carry with poor stammering lips the word of salvation to the scattered sheep of the House of Israel; still I do long, if it be the Lord's will, to feed once more the flock that was given me in the dew of my youth. Whether I shall be permitted—and how long—to take up so great a work again, my Master only knows. But if you wish for it as fervently as I do, solemnly agree in the presence of God, on the night on which this letter is read to you, to these two things: (1) Strive together with me in your prayers to God for me, that it would please Him to forgive and forget our past sins and shortcomings—mine in carrying the message and yours in receiving it—and that He would really heal my body and strengthen my soul for again uptaking the blessed work of the ministry among you, and that He would grant us a prosperous journey to come unto you. (2) Solemnly agree, in the strength of the Lord Jesus, to "break off your sins by righteousness, and your iniquities by showing mercy to the poor." The sin of one Achan troubles the whole camp of Israel. If any one of you who are

God's children wilfully continue in some old sin, then it may be God will for your sake trouble our camp and continue His chastening. See that no fleshly lust, no covetousness, which is idolatry, no hankering after the world and its unholy pleasures, no unlawful affection, be reigning in you. Clean out the old leaven from all your houses, so we may meet again in peace and be refreshed together by days of the Lord's presence and of the Spirit's power such as we have never seen before. This is the heart's desire and prayer of your affectionate pastor, Robert Murray McCheyne.

Dated: *Breslau in Prussia, 16 October, 1839*

Also available from Kingsley Press

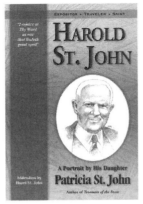

If you enjoy reading about the lives of great Christians, you'll love this biography of Harold St. John. His daughter, Patricia St. John, did the Christian world an enormous favor when she put together this fascinating portrait of her father. Somehow her portrayal manages to be exciting, inspiring, challenging, amusing and edifying all at the same time. It makes compelling reading from start to finish—hard to put down once you've picked it up. Harold was one of the most gifted Bible teachers of his day, and the story of his life and influence is as relevant now as ever. His life was hid with Christ in God, and out of his inward parts there flowed a river of joy and peace and blessedness that enriched everyone it touched. *172 pages*

Check out our web site for details of other publications and online ordering.

www.kingsleypress.com

Alternatively, you may write to the address at the front of this book.